WILD WORK

Who Walks the Tightrope?
WORKING AT A CIRCUS

Mary Meinking

Chicago, Illinois

www.heinemannraintree.com

Visit our website to find out more information about Heinemann-Raintree books.

To order:

☎ Phone 888-454-2279

🖥 Visit www.heinemannraintree.com to browse our catalog and order online.

Edited by David Andrews, Nancy Dickmann, and Rebecca Rissman
Designed by Victoria Allen
Picture research by Liz Alexander
Leveled by Marla Conn, with Read-Ability.
Originated by Dot Gradations Ltd
Printed and bound in China by Leo Paper Products Ltd

15 14 13 12 11 10
10 9 8 7 6 5 4 3 2 1

Library of Congress Cataloging-in-Publication Data
Meinking, Mary.
 Who walks the tightrope? : working at a circus / Mary Meinking.
  p. cm.—(Wild work)
 Includes bibliographical references and index.
 ISBN 978-1-4109-3852-7 (hc)—ISBN 978-1-4109-3861-9 (pb) 1. Circus—Juvenile literature. 2. Circus performers—Vocational guidance—United States—Juvenile literature.
I. Title.
 GV1817.C47 2011
 791.3023—dc22   2009050289

J-nf

Acknowledgements

The author and publisher are grateful to the following for permission to reproduce copyright material:

Alamy pp. **7** (© Ambient Images Inc), **12** (© Agripicture Images), **13** (© picturesbyrob), **17** (© tony French), **20** (© RubberBall), **24** (© ClassicStock), **29** (© Picture Contact); Corbis pp. **5** (© Steve Marcus), **10** (© John Lund), **15** (© Henry Diltz), **16** (© Tom Fox/Dallas Morning News), **18** (© Juan Medina/Reuters), **19** (© Aristide Economopoulos/Star Ledger); Getty Images pp **8** (Pascal Guyot/AFP), **9** (Zigy Kaluzny/Stone), **11** (Darren McCollester), **14** (Ian Shaw/Stone), **25** (Stan Honda/AFP), **26** (Monaco Centre de Presse-pool), **28** (Sandra Mu); Guinness World Records Smashed on Sky 1/ Andi Southam p. **21**; Photolibrary pp. **6** (White), **22** (L SA House - Willinger/Superstock), **23** (Motor-Presse Syndication/ Superstock), **27** (Robert Ginn/Index Stock Imagery); Shutterstock p. **4** (© Losevsky Pavel).

Background design features reproduced with permission of Shutterstock (© hcreate).

Cover photograph reproduced with permission of TopFoto (©RIA Novosti).

Every effort has been made to contact copyright holders of any material reproduced in this book. Any omissions will be rectified in subsequent printings if notice is given to the publisher.

Disclaimer

Some words are shown in bold, **like this.** You can find out what they mean by looking in the glossary.

3 9547 00357 2240

Contents

Under the Big Top

Step right up for a sneak peek at the circus! **Performers** fly through the air. Others tie themselves in knots. Many circuses move from town to town.

A modern kind of circus is called a **cirque** (say *SURK*). People perform in these circuses. The performers' acts often tell a story.

Step Right Up!

The **ringmaster** keeps the show going.
He or she tells which act is next.
Ringmasters talk about the danger
or special talent of each act.

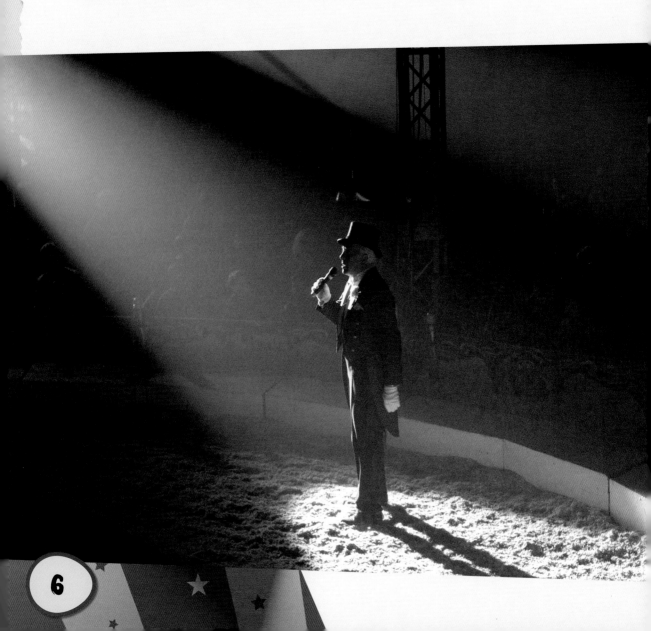

Most **performers** don't speak during the show. The ringmaster speaks for them. Some ringmasters act along with the performers.

Walking on Air

High in the air, tightrope walkers move along a wire. Many walkers carry a pole to help them keep their balance. Some do **somersaults** on the wire. Others juggle or do tricks as a group.

tightrope

DID YOU KNOW?

Tightrope walkers wear thin shoes so their feet can grab the wire.

Flying High

A pair of **trapeze** artists swing high above the crowd. One hangs by his knees. The other slides off her trapeze and does flips in the air. Her partner catches her.

trapeze

Other **aerialists** (say *AIR-ee-uh-lists*) perform on a fabric rope hanging from the ceiling. They climb, swing, and spin on the rope.

What Daredevils!

Daredevils do dangerous things to amaze the crowds. Human **cannonballs** are shot out of cannons. There's no explosion—a blast of air shoots them out. They land safely in a net or on a huge bag of air.

DID YOU KNOW?

Human cannonballs fly faster than some cars go!

Fire **performers** eat fire, breathe fire, or juggle things that are on fire. They know the secrets of doing fire tricks so they don't get burned. Sword swallowers shock crowds with their tricks.

You're not a circus performer. So don't try these tricks at home!

Tossed in the Air

Circus jugglers toss almost anything. Most use balls, rings, or clubs. Some juggle flaming torches or chainsaws.

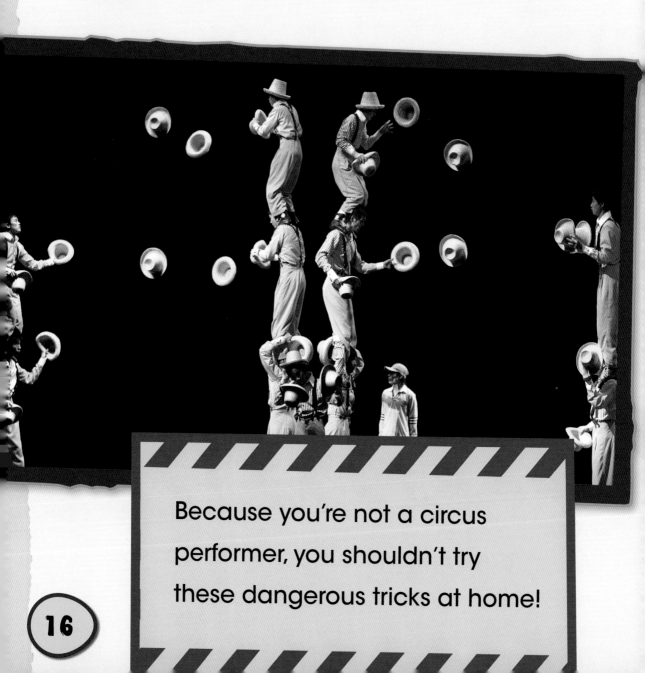

Because you're not a circus performer, you shouldn't try these dangerous tricks at home!

Jugglers start off with three things. Then more are added. Some jugglers work as a team passing things back and forth.

Tied in Knots

Can you stretch your legs behind your head? Then you're born to be a **contortionist** (say *con-TORE-shon-ist*). These **performers** stretch a lot so they can bend into strange shapes.

Some contortionists can squeeze into a box the size of a microwave. Others can squeeze through an unstrung tennis racket.

DID YOU KNOW?

In May 2009 a **contortionist** named Iona Luvsandorj did a back bend for 33 seconds. She held herself up with only her mouth!

Clowning Around

Clowns make people laugh by doing funny **skits** or tricks. There are many kinds of clowns. Whiteface clowns wear white makeup and look sad.

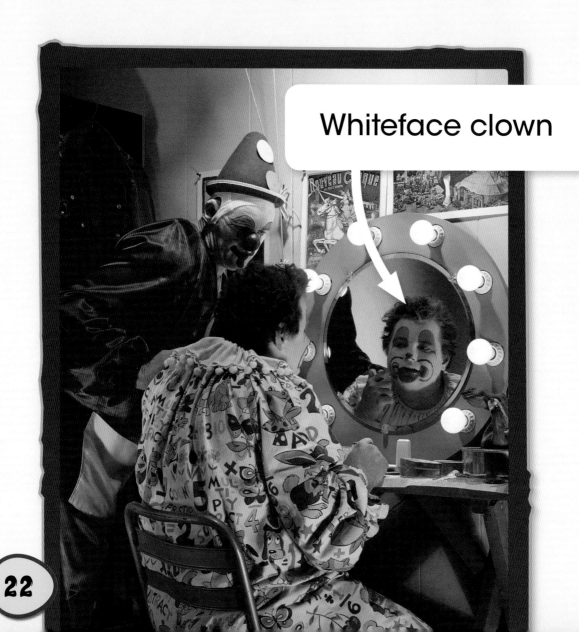

Whiteface clown

Auguste (say *ah-GUST*) clowns have a big mouth and eyes and wear bright clothes. Character clowns wear beards and torn clothes.

Every clown is different. They go to a special school to learn how to become clowns. In clown school they decide what kind of clown they'll be. They choose their clown name, clothes, and makeup, and practice their acts.

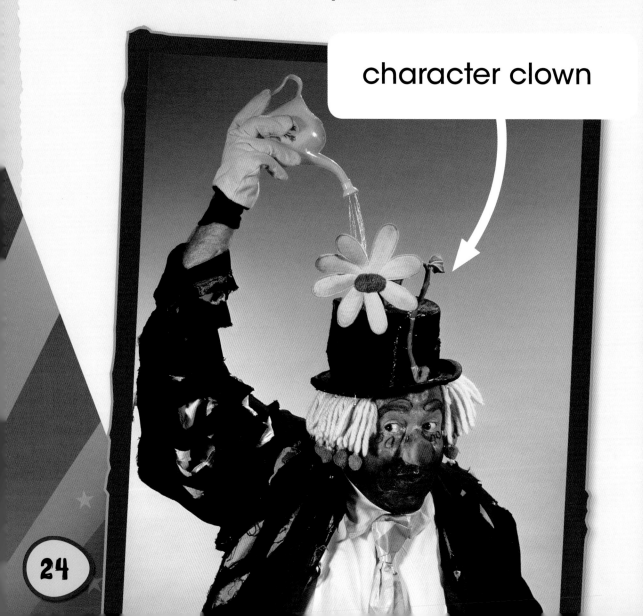

character clown

Fun Fact: Joeys Everywhere

Joseph "Joey" Grimaldi was a clown in England in the early 1800s. He became famous. Clowns today are sometimes called "Joeys" after him.

Animal Show

Some circuses have animal acts. Good circuses treat their animals well.

Circus staff feed and clean the animals. **Veterinarians** help if an animal gets sick or injured. They keep the animals healthy.

Could You Work in a Circus?

Do you want to be a circus **performer**? They exercise and practice every day. They can't be shy in front of crowds.

Children perform in circuses too. They still have to do homework at night. Circuses are away from home most of the year. The circus staff becomes their family.

Glossary

aerialist person who performs in the air

cannonball a round object shot from a cannon

cirque modern circus that tells a story

contortionist person who can bend their body into extreme positions

daredevil person who performs dangerous tricks

performer person who does something in front of a crowd

ringmaster person who announces the circus acts

skit a short, funny act

somersault tumbling head over feet

trapeze a swing held high in the air

veterinarian animal doctor

Find Out More

Books to Read

Jordan, Denise. *Circus Performers*. Chicago: Heinemann-Raintree, 2002.

Robertson, Patrisha. *Cirque du Soleil: A Parade of Colors*. New York: Harry N. Abrams, 2003.

Web Sites

http://www.ringling.com/TopLanding.aspx?id=11610
This web site features circus games, puzzles and quizzes. It also tells about circus history and fun facts.

http://learnhowtojuggle.info
This site shows step-by-step how to juggle. It includes pictures to follow along.

http://www.carrsonbarnescircus.com
This site includes information and a video on circus animal care.

Index